SARDAR PATEL
IN
CARTOONS

SARDAR PATEL
IN
CARTOONS

Chief Editor
P. N. CHOPRA
Editor
PRABHA CHOPRA

RELIANCE PUBLISHING HOUSE
NEW DELHI

Cataloging in Publication Data--DK
Courtesy: D.K. Agencies (P) Ltd. <docinfo@dkagencies.com>

Sardar Patel in cartoons / chief editor, P.N. Chopra ; editor, Prabha Chopra.
xxviii, 105 p.
Vallabhbhai Patel, 1875-1950, Indian statesman.
ISBN 8175101954

1. Patel, Vallabhbhai, 1875-1950.--Caricatures and cartoons. 2. Statesmen--India--Caricatures and cartoons. 3. Nationalists--India--Caricatures and cartoons. I. Chopra, P. N. (Pran Nath), 1926- II. Chopra, Prabha, 1931-

DDC 954.035 022 2 21

First Published 2005

ISBN : 81-7510-195-4

Price : Rs. 195/-

Published by
Dr. S.K. Bhatia
(Life Member Common Cause HWF, ILA & INSA Lions Clubs Int.)
for **RELIANCE PUBLISHING HOUSE**
3026/7H, Ranjit Nagar, New Delhi-110 008
Ph. : 25847377 / 25842605 Fax : 25842605

Composed by
Elegant Printographics
319, R. G. Complex, IIIrd Floor,
Sector-14, Rohini, Delhi-110085
Ph. : 27567413

Printed by :
S.S.S. Printers
New Delhi.

Preface

Sardar Vallabhbhai Patel ranks as one of the foremost leaders of India alongwith Gandhiji and Jawaharlal Nehru. These three leaders were mainly responsible for giving shape to the destiny of the Country during the freedom struggle and in the early years after the attainment of independence. Gandhiji inspired his countrymen for the independence of the country, Nehru formulated the foreign policy and Sardar Patel unified the country into one united whole in a remarkable manner.

A man of Iron will Sardar Patel, as Minister incharge of States, dealt with the complex question of 560 and odd princely states in a masterly manner and almost within a year, he redrew the map of India with every such state joining the Indian Union and forming a part of the political and cultural life of the mainstream. It is a feat unparalled in the history of the world. V. Shankar, Sardar Patel's Principal Secretary rightly observed "Today, whatever may be disruptive forces that threaten the country, the political solidarity and integrity established by Sardar's statesmanship still holds". Even if the Sardar had not done anything else other than this unification of the country, his name would have been written in letters of gold in Indian history.

After consolidation of the Country by merging the five hundred sixty and odd princely states in the Indian Uniion, Sardar's attention was focussed on consolidating the economy of the country by ensuring maximum production. He advocated liberalisation. On the administrative side he brought out reforms in **"The Steel Frame"** as the "Indian Civil Services" was called which was disrupted during partition. He evolved two new services viz. The Indian Administrative Services and Indian Police Services to take place of former "Indian Civil Service" and Indian Police Services and advised them to maintain "highest standard of integrity".

Sardar Patel Society, with Late Shri S. Nijalingappa, as its founder President and former Chief Minister of Karnataka and Dr. P.N. Chopra and Dr. (Mrs.) Prabha Chopra as its Member-Secretary and Secretary respectively, has brought out since its inception in 1989, fifteen volumes of "Collected Works of Sardar Patel"; his daughter Maniben Patel's Diary; a biography of Sardar Patel; his photographic Album and a few thematic volumes viz. Sardar Patel — Kashmir & Hyderabad; Sardar Patel — Muslims and Refugees; Sardar Patel–Economy and Foreign Policy; Sardar Patel and his relations with Gandhi, Nehru and Subhas etc.

The present volume on "Sardar Patel in Cartoons" is another singular effort to present Sardar Patel through a Cartoonist's eyes. Cartoonists have become an integral part of the intellectual life of today's society. A Cartoonist is not simply a fun maker but one who notices the significance of an event and by some master strokes impresses it on others.

We are obliged to Nehru Memorial Museum and Library for extending to us all the help to collect these Cartoons from various News Papers from the period of actual participation of Sardar Patel in Public and Political Life till his death in 1950. Our thanks are due to Mrs. Poonam Surie for collection of material from the above sources. We are grateful to Hindustan Times management for allowing us to publish the Cartoons which appeared in their esteemed daily from 1945 to 1950. Our thanks are also due to Shri M.P. Chawla, Accounts Officer and Shri

Rabindra Kumar Das who took pains in sifting thc Cartoons, arranging them chronologically and accurately and promptly typing out the material. We should like to expresss our thanks to M/s. Reliance Publishing House for undertaking its publication.

P.N. Chopra
(*Chief Editor*)
Prabha Chopra
(*Editor*)

List of Sardar Patel in Cartoon

Sr. No.	*Title*	*Sources*	*Page No.*
1.	"The Camel and the Merchant's Tent"	The Hindustan Times June 21, 1945	1
2.	"The Man of the Moment" - Asked if he would fccl happpy to join the Viceroy's Excutive Council, Pandit Jawaharlal Nehru stated that it would depend on his mood at the moment	The Hindustan Times July 3, 1945	2
3.	"Tips to Vanishing Suns" - Sir A.R. Mudaliar was named "Chief Running Sun" when he visited the "Black-feet" Indian tribe in Glacier National Park in Montana.	The Hindustan Times July, 7, 1945	3
4.	"Undertakers All"	The Hindustan Times July 14, 1945	4
5.	"And the Sea Gave up the Dead..." (Wavell Plan)	The Hindustan Times July 17, 1945	5
6.	"Still Surplus; Have Another" - Baroda Budget was presented to the State Assembly. It is a balanced budget with a surplus of Rs. 30,000/- A.P.I. Report	The Hindustan Times July 26, 1945	6

Sr. No.	Title	Sources	Page No.
7.	"How They Fought and Won" - Sir A. Ramaswami Mudaliar has returned to Delhi (And the Big Wolf would have killed all of us)	The Hindustant Times August 1, 1945	7
8.	"Once a Soldier, Always a Soldier" - The Modern Soldier is certainly more capable of adapting himself to new weapons and new conditions than the old type would have been - Lord Wavell on "The Good Soldier".	The Hindustan Times August 22, 1945	8
9.	"Protect us, Brother" - Raksha Bandhan is being celebrated in India	The Hindustan Times August 23, 1945	9
10.	"Lease or Lend" - 12 men were kept awake for 112 hours for testing the effects of insomnia on human beings at the California Institute of Technology in U.S.A. India can easily lend the services of many men who have not had a wink of sleep after Lord Wavell's departure for London.	The Hindustan Times Sept. 5, 1945	10
11.	"Willingly, If you Will" - The Finance Department is reported to have taken up the	The Hindustan Times September 14, 1945	11

Sr. No.	Title	Sources	Page No.
	question of retrenchment. Why not start at the top.		
12.	"You Don't Mean us?" - A Government of India Gazette Extra ordinary says: "The War Watching and Coast Watching Services will be disbanded"	The HindustanTimes Nov. 27, 1945	12
13.	"Freedom to Freeze" - We are going through a very difficult and testing time, and it will need coolness if we are to avoid calamity. In so far as I can help by personal contact, I am always prepared to do so" - Lord Wavell.	The HindustanTimes December 11, 1945	13
14.	"March of Time" (Text below the Cartoons)	The Hindustan Times March 17, 1946	14
15.	"Congrophobia" - "Is this the atmosphere or situation which one can consider as being conducive to the opening of negotiation between two major nations in this country?" - Jinnah on the Cabinet Mission.	The Hindustan Times March 20, 1946	15
16.	"Self Help, Best Help" - In campaigning armed private defenceagainst violence by	The Times of India March 26, 1946	16

Sr. No.	Title	Sources	Page No.
	political or communal bodies, the European Asson. says that the objects in view are not confirmed to the British Community alone but to help all peaceful individuals when faced with a menacing situation, beyond the reach of law and order.		
17.	"March of Time" (Text Below)	The Hindustan Times March 31, 1946	17
18.	"Handsome is that Handsome - Does" Sir Ramaswami Mudaliar said during the food debate in the Assembly that there was no lack of sympathy in the United States, But their administrative machinery was faulty. Will the Government of India lend a helping hand?	The Hindustan Times April 3, 1946	18
19.	"The People's Theatre" - The importance of the Central Assembly session is eclipsed by the Cabinet Mission deliberations and the attendance is falling steadily. Members might imitate I.P.T.A. activities and make the session lively.	The Hindustan Times April 6, 1946	19

Sr. No.	Title	Sources	Page No.
20.	"Hatching Season" - The Cabinet Mission is Going out of Delhi on a holiday to Kashmir and wishes not to be followed.	The Hindustan Times April 10, 1946	20
21.	"Look who Backs us;" - Sir Firoz Khan Noon in an interview said that Russia would help the Muslims in India if their demand for Pakistan is not conceded.	The Hindustan Times April 13, 1946	21
22.	"March of Time" (Text Below)	The Hindustan Times April 21, 1946	22
23.	"The haves and Have Nots" (News Ration Shop Simla)	The Hindustan Times May 9, 1946	23
24.	"Strictly Confidential"	The Hindustan Times May 11, 1946	24
25.	"March of Time" (Text Below)	The Hindustan Times May 12, 1946	25
26.	"Wait and Watch"	The Hindustan Times May 22, 1946	26
27.	"Catch'em All and Catch'em quick" - The Indian States will become independent, units when British India gets independence and the British	The Hindustan Times May 24, 1946.	27

Sr. No.	Title	Sources	Page No.
	Government could not, and will not transfer para mountry to an Indian Government, says a Press Note issued by the Cabinet Mission.		
28.	"March of Time" (Text Below)	The Hindustan Times May 26, 1946	28
29.	"Say Encores" That the Cabinet Mission's latest statement, clarifying certain points leaves the position where it was, is the opinion held in Congress circles in New Delhi, according to an Agency message.	The Hindustan Times May 28, 1946	29
30.	"Heat Wave Again in Delhi"	The Hindustan Times June 5, 1946	30
31.	"Accused that Delivers Judgement" Sir Edward Benthall, War Transport Member, stated at a Press Conference at Calcutta that the Government of India must retain in its hand the ultimate control in connection with the Adjudicator's award and the Government was the final judge in the matter."	The Hindustan Times June 11, 1946	31

Sr. No.	Title	Sources	Page No.
32.	"A little Sacrifice, Please;"	The Hindustan Times June 14, 1946	32
33.	"Try, Try, Try Again"	The Hindustan Times June 15, 1946	33
34.	"Scorched Earth Plan" - The National Planning Committee has condemned the Government's action in abolishing the Planning Deptt.	The Hindustan Times July 11, 1946	34
35.	"March of Time" (Text Below)	The Hindustan Times July 21, 1946	35
36.	"Direct Action Begins;"- Mr. Churchil Leader of the opposition in the House of Commons, is reported to be taking steps to oppose the Labour Government's India policy.	The Hindustan Times August 4, 1946	36
37.	"Darkness All Round"- ... I am afraid the situation remains as it was and we are where we were." - Jinnah.	The Hindustan Times August 14, 1946	37
38.	"Help, Help; They're Planning to Sink us"-"It is quite clear that the intervention of the Viceroy is being sought to over throw the League	The Hindustan Times September 10, 1946	38

Sr. No.	Title	Sources	Page No.
	Ministry by alienating the sympathy of its supporters" - Hidayatullah		
39.	"Cold Weather Pests - I" (Text Below)	The Hindustan Times November 26, 1946	39
40.	"Imaginary Stumbling - Block" - As the talks appeared to be nearingtheir end, Mr. Attlee succeeded in bringing the Indian leaders together with Britain's representatives at a round table conference.	The Hindustan Times December 8, 1946	40
41.	"Going My Way?" - "I visualize a time when no Muslim will be in the Congress at no distant future and when that time comes we shall have to acknowledge our debt to Sardar Patel. The plight of Nationalist Muslims is rapidly becoming intolerable." - Raja Ghazanfar Ali.	The Hindustan Times December 12, 1946	41
42.	"Non-Stop to Independence" (Text Below)	The Hindustan Times December 18, 1946	42
43.	"First Aid ..... Last Aid?'	The Hindustan Times February 4, 1947	43

Sr. No.	Title	Sources	Page No.
44.	"Rendered Innocuous"	The Hindustan Times March 27, 1947	44
45.	"Chalti Dunya" - Magazine Section (Text Below)	The Hindustan Times June 8, 1947	45
46.	"Tree Planting" - Delhi's Tree Planting Week Commences today with a demonstration of Tree-Planting organized by the Deputy Commissioner, in the grounds of Purana Qila.	The Hindustan Times June 20, 1947	46
47.	"Chalti Dunya" - Magazine Section (Text Below)	The Hindustan Times June 29, 1947	47
48.	"The Sun, The Moon and the Flying Saucers"- We do not propose to recognize the States as separate international entities on August 15th. - Sir Hartley Shawcross.	The Hindustan Times July 17, 1947	48
49.	"Punch - And - Judy Show" - Sir C.P. Ramaswamy Iyer again met Lord Mountbatten on Tuesday.	The Hindustan Times July 24, 1947	49
50.	"May We Come In Now?" - Travancore has decided to accede to the Indian Dominion.	The Hindustan Times July 31, 1947	50

Sr. No.	Title	Sources	Page No.
51.	"To Those Who Serve" - Congress leaders will be blessed by Delhi ladies prior to their departure for the Constituent Assembly on the night of August 14, by marking "Mangal Tilak" on their foreheads.	The Hindustan Times August 14, 1947	51
52.	"Out of the Wilderness"	The Hindustan Times August 15, 1947	52
53.	"Those Who Have Led The Nation To Independence"	The Hindustan Times August 15, 1947	53
54.	"Chalti Dunya" - Magazine Section (Text Below)	The Hindustan Times August 17, 1947	55
55.	"With These Rings...;" - The Committee on minorities report was dabated in the Constituent Assembly and the motion for joint Electorates was passed unanimously."	The Hindustan Times August 29, 1947	56
56.	"Chalti Dunya" - Magazine Section (Text Below)	The Hindustan Times August 31, 1947	57
57.	"The Leopard Changes Its Spots" - a change in the attitude of the Hyderabad Delegation is believed to have	The Hindustan Times October 14, 1947	58

Sr. No.	Title	Sources	Page No.
	given a hopeful turn to the negotiations now proceeding.		
58.	"Chalti Dunya" - Magazine Section (Text Below)	The Hindustan Times Octobe 19, 1947	59
59.	"Didn't You See How He Tried To Bite Me?" - Mr. Jinnah's latest telegram to the Ruler of Kashmir accuses the State authorities of opening fire on Pakistan Troops.	The Hindustan Times October 28, 1947	60
60.	"Chalti Dunya" - Magazine Section (Text Below)	The Hindustan Times November 2, 1947	61
61.	"Waiter;" - "If he still wants it he can come and get it himself."	The Hindustan Times June 30, 1948	62
62.	"That Attitude of Yours will Get You Really Nowhere;"	Hindustan Times July 21, 1948	63
63.	"A Sore on the Elephant's Back"	The Hindustan Times August 7, 1948	64
64.	"Chalti Dunya" - Magazine Section (Text Below)	The Hindustan Times October 31, 1947	65
65.	"Chalti Dunya" - Magazine Section (Text Below)	The Hindustan Times November 31, 1947	66

Sr. No.	Title	Sources	Page No.
66.	"The Newest Look" - The Soviet Government newspaper claims that the Presidium of the National Congress has taken secret decision on dual citizenship for Indians, both Indian and British.	The Hindustan Times November 23, 1948	67
67.	"Santhanam's Travel Agency" (You've seen Nothing Till You've Seen - India) - "India has managed to cling to unique traditions of dress, etc." - Mr. K. Santhanam.	The Hindustan Times November 30, 1948	68
68.	"Whither?" (Dark Forest of National Bondage)	The Hindustan Times December 18, 1948	69
69.	"A Tale Come True - 1885 to 1948"	The Hindustan Times (Supplement to H.T.) December 18, 1948	70
70.	"Chalti Dunya" - Magazine Section	The Hindustan Times December 19, 1948	71
71.	"Chalti Dunya" - Magazine Section	The Hindustan Times January 30, 1949	72
72.	"Chalti Dunya" - Magazine Section	The Hindustan Times February 13, 1949	73
73.	"Good Boys; Move up To the Top of the Class".	The Hindustan Times February 24, 1949	74

Sr. No.	Title	Sources	Page No.
74.	"Chalti Dunya" - Magazine Section	The Hindustan Times March 6, 1949	75
75.	"No Horse-Sense;"	The Hindustan Times March 8, 1949	76
76.	"Chalti Dunya" - Magazine Section	The Hindustan Times March 13, 1949	77
77.	"Chalti Dunya" - Magazine Section	The Hindustan Times March 20, 1949	78
78.	"Chalti Dunya" - Magazine Section	The Hindustan Times April 10, 1949	79
79.	"Onward, Commonwealth Soldiers;" - It should not be difficult to fit a Republic into the framework of the "Commonwealth", Pandit Nehru told a "Daily Mail" corres-pondent. On the question of Commonwealth deference he said: "It would not be in the interests of India to engage herself in any pact that would automatically involve her in war."	The Hindustan Times April 13, 1949	80
80.	"Achievement"	The Hindustan Times May 7, 1949	81

Sr. No.	*Title*	*Sources*	*Page No.*
81.	"Chalti Dunya" - Magazine Section	The Hindustan Times May 22, 1949	82
82.	"Chalti Dunya" - Magazine Section	The Hindustan Times June 12, 1949	83
83.	"Chalti Dunya" - Magazine Section	The Hindustan Times June 12, 1949	84
84.	"Lest We Forget;" (Aug 15 1948 to Aug. 15, 1949 A Year of Achievement)	The Hindustan Times August 15, 1948-1949	85
85.	"Attention Boys" - If we reflect deeper on the problems that face us, I find no room for despair or despondency: If, for a moment, we reflect on the problems which we have successfully faced, the difficulties which we have effectiely countered and the obligations which we have faithfully discharged, I have no doubt we shall see rays of ligh which would penetrate through the gloom which surrounds us and would fill us with hope and courage" says Sardar Patel in his Independence Days Massage to the Nation.	The Hindustan Times August 17; 1949	86

Sr. No.	***Title***	***Sources***	***Page No.***
86.	"Riding Instructors?"	The Hindustan Times October 12, 1949	87
87.	"Chalti Dunya" - Magazine Section	The Hindustan Times October 16, 1949	88
88.	"Gulliver Gets a Break"	The Hindustan Times November 16, 1949	89
89.	"Chalti Dunya" - Magazine Section	The Hindustan Times November 20, 1949	90
90.	"Chalti Dunya" - Magazine Section (Sunday Weekly)	The Hindustan Times February 5, 1950	91
91.	"None so Blind As They That Will Not See"	The Hindustan Times April 18, 1950	92
92.	"Chalti Dunya" - Magazine Section	The Hindustan Times April 30, 1950	93
93.	"White washed"	The Hindustan Times May 5, 1950	94
94.	"Three-Year-Old Sapling"	The Hindustan Times August 15, 1950	95
95.	"Chalti Dunya" - Magazine Section	The Hindustan Times August 20, 1950	96
96.	"Steel Frame" Liquidation and After	The Bombay Chronicle January 16, 1947	97

Sr. No.	*Title*	*Sources*	*Page No.*
97.	Tug of (Cold) War	The Bombay Chronicle June 23, 1948	98
98.	The Lunatic At Large	The Bombay Chronicle July 2, 1948	99
99.	Peace Seeker	The Bombay Chronicle August 6, 1948	100
100.	Gulliver Awakes	The Bombay Chronicle August 11, 1948	101
101.	Appearance and Reality	The Bombay Chronicle February 24, 1949	102
102.	"Your'e Welcome ...	The Bombay Chronicle April 11, 1949	103
103.	The Hall of Fame	The Bombay Chronicle May 9, 1949	104
104.	Hats Off to New Order	The Bombay Chronicle May 30, 1949	105

THE CAMEL AND THE MERCHANT'S TENT

The Hindustan Times, Thursday, June 21, 1945.

THE MAN OF THE MOMENT

Asked if he would feel happy to join the Viceroy's Executive Council, Pandit Jawaharlal Nehru stated that it would depend on his mood at the moment.

The Hindustan Times, Tuesday, July 3, 1945.

TIPS TO VANISHING SUNS

Sir A. R. Mudaliar was named "Chief Running Sun" when he visited the "Black-feet" Indian tribe in Glacier National Park in Montana.

The Hindustan Times, Saturday, July 7, 1945.

UNDERTAKERS ALL

The Hindustan Times, Saturday, July 14, 1945.

"AND THE SEA GAVE UP THE DEAD—"

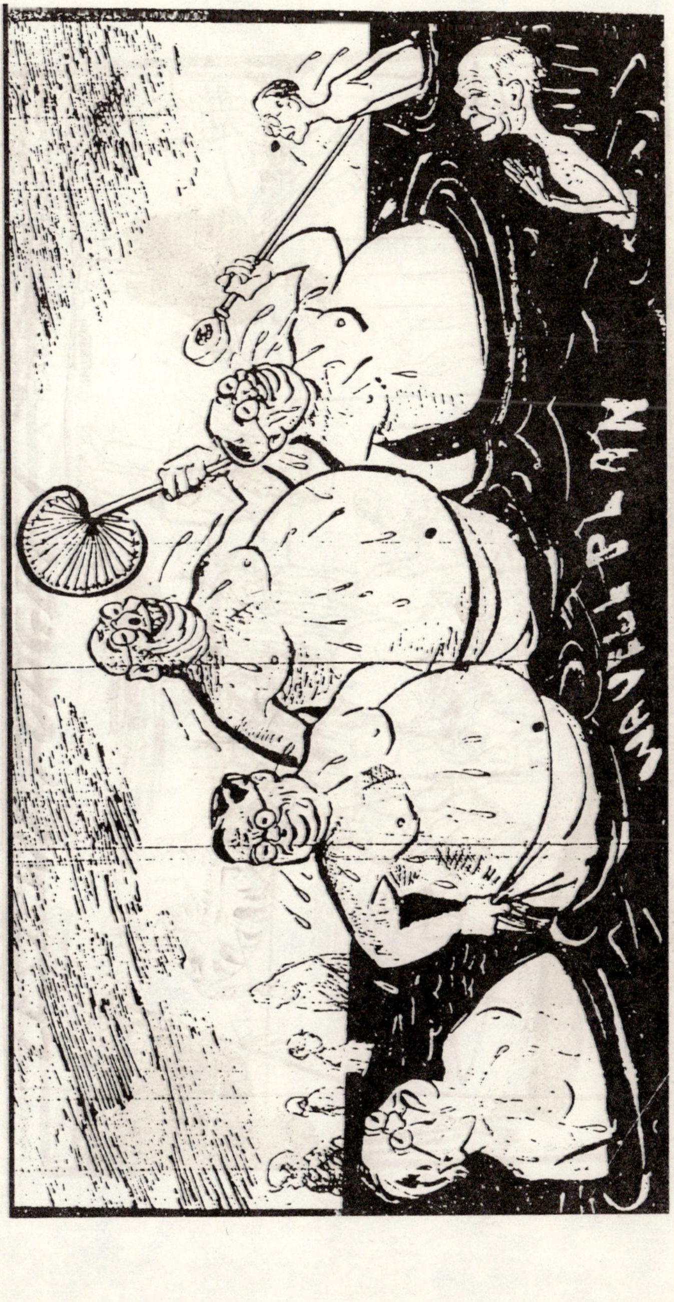

The Hindustan Times, Tuesday, July 17, 1945.

STILL SURPLUS! HAVE ANOTHER

Baroda Budget was presented to the State Assembly. It is a balanced budget with a surplus of Rs. 30,000/-..
The Hindustan Times, Thursday, July 26, 1945

HOW THEY FOUGHT AND WON

Sir A. Ramaswami Mudaliar has returned to Delhi.
The Hindustan Times, Tuesday, August 1, 1945.

ONCE A SOLDIER, ALWAYS A SOLDIER

The modern soldier is certainly more capable of adapting himself to new weapons and new conditions than the old type would have been. Lord Wavell on "The Good Soldier".

The Hindustan Times, Wednesday, August 22, 1945.

'PROTECT US, BROTHER'

Raksha Bandhan is being celebrated in India.

The Hindustan Times, Thursday, August 23, 1945.

LEASE OR LEND

12 men were kept awake for 112 hours for testing the effects of insomnia on human beings at the California Institute of Technology in U.S.A. India can easily lend the services of many men who have not had a wink of sleep after Lord Wavell's departure for London.

The Hindustan Times, Wednesday, September 5, 1945

WILLINGLY, IF YOU WILL

The Finance Department is reported to have taken up the question of retrenchment. Why not start at the top.

The Hindustan Times, Friday, September 14, 1945.

YOU DON'T MEAN US?

A Government of India Gazette Extraordinary says : "The War Watching and Coast Watching Services will be disbanded."

The Hindustan Times, Tuesday, November 27, 1945.

FREEDOM TO FREEZE

We are going through a very difficult and testing time and it will need coolness if we are to avoid calamity. In so far as I can help by personal contact, I am always prepared to do so : Lord Wavell

The Hindustan Times, Tuesday, December 11, 1945

MARCH OF TIME

The Hindustan Times, Wednesday, March 17, 1946

CONGROPHOBIA

"Is this the atmosphere or situation which one can consider as being conducive to the opening of negotiation between two major nations in this country?" — **Jinnah** on the Cabinet Mission

The Hindustan Times, Wednesday, March 20, 1946.

The Hindustan Times, Wednesday, March 20, 1946.

SELF HELP, BEST HELP

In campaining armed private defence against violence by political or communal bodies, the European Association says that the objects in view are not confined to the British community alone, but to help all peaceful individuals when faced with a menacing situation, beyond the reach of law and order.

The Hindustan Times, Tuesday, March 26, 1946.

MARCH OF TIME

The Hindustan Times, March 31, 1946.

HANDSOME IS THAT HANDSOME DOES

Sir Ramaswami Madaliar said during the Food debate in the Assembly that there was no lack of sympathy in the United States, but their administrative machinery was faulty. Will the Governement of India lend a helping hand?

The Hindustan Times, Wednesday, April 3, 1946.

THE PEOPLE'S THEATRE

The importance of the Central Assembly session is eclipsed by the Cabinet Mission deliberations and the attendance is falling staedily. Members might imitate I.-P.T.A. activities and make the session lively.

The Hindustan Times, Saturday, April 6, 1946.

HATCHING SEASON

The Cabinet Mission is going out of Delhi on a holiday to Kashmir and wishes not to be followed.
The Hindustan Times, Wednesday, April 10, 1946.

LOOK WHO BACKS US

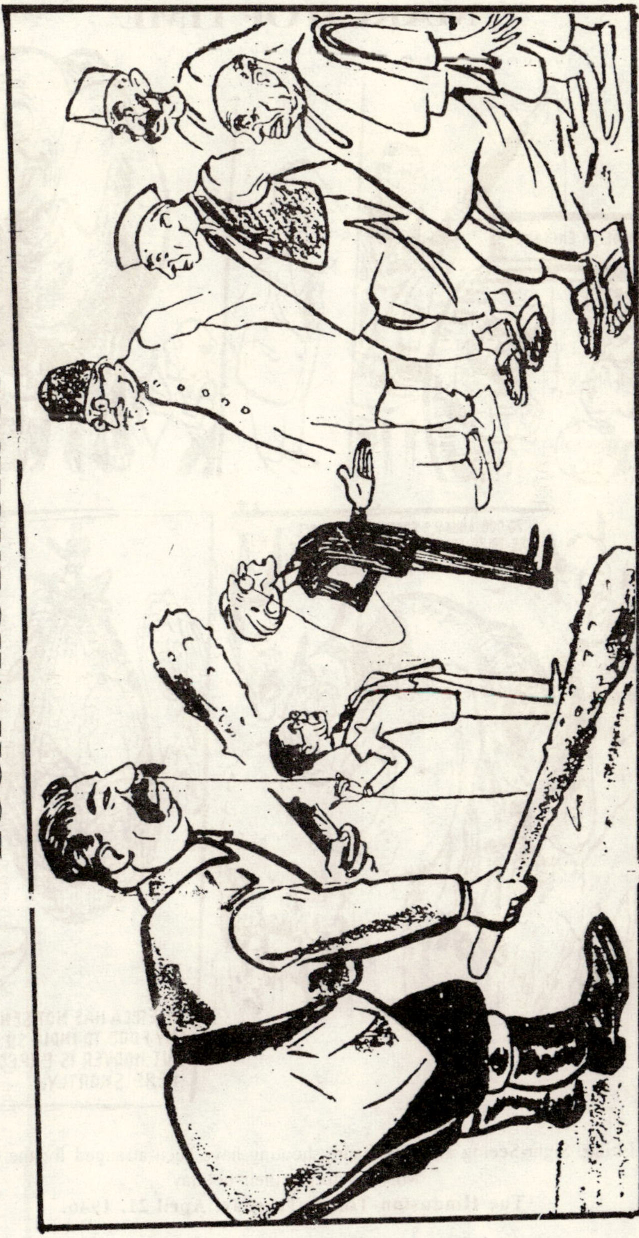

Sir Firoz Khan Noon in an interview said that Russia would help the Muslims in India if their demand for Pakistan is not corceded.

The Hindustan Times, Saturday, April 13, 1946.

MARCH OF TIME

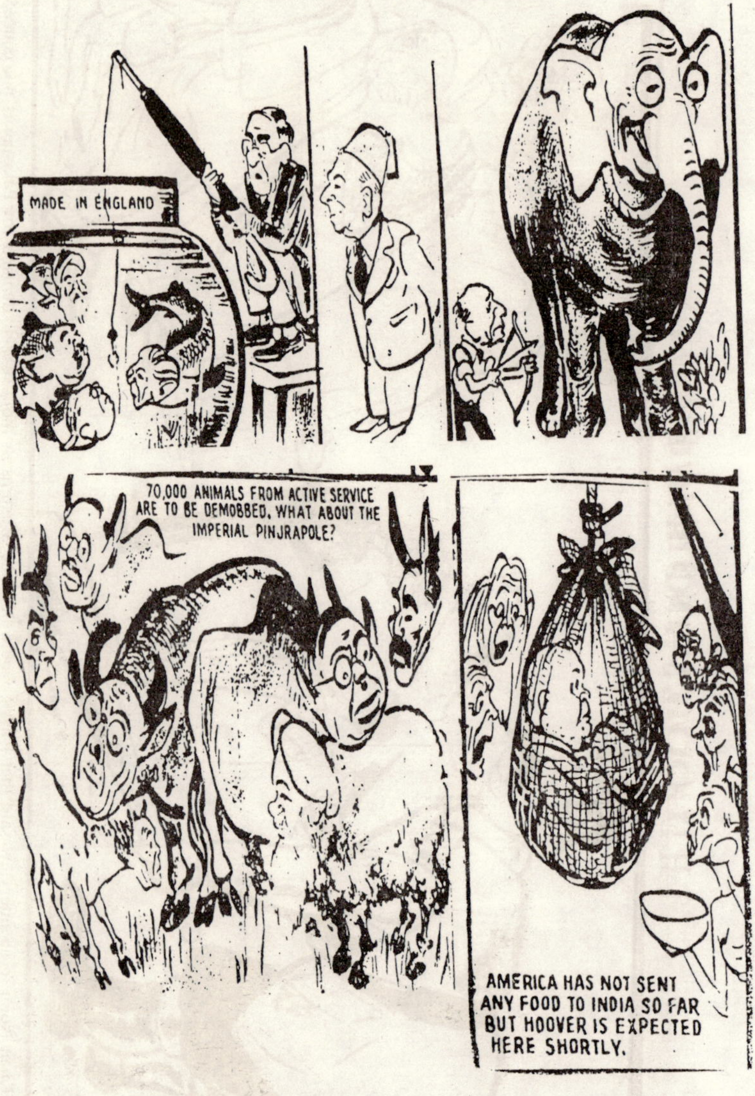

Fishing, Sight-Seeing and Big Game shooting have been arranged for the cabinet Mission during their holiday.

The Hindustan Times, Tuesday, April 21, 1946.

THE HAVES AND HAVE NOTS

The Hindustan Times, Thursday, May 9, 1946.

STRICTLY CONFIDENTIAL

The Hindustan Times, Saturday, May 11, 1946.

MARCH OF TIME

The Hindustan Times, May 12, 1946.

WAIT AND WATCH

The Hindustan Times, Wednesday, May 22, 1946.

CATCH'EM ALL AND CATCH'EM QUICK

The Indian States will become independent units when British India gets independence, and the British Government could not, and will not transfer paramountry to an Indian Government, says a Press Note issued by the Cabinet Mission.

The Hindustan Times, Friday, May 24, 1946

Just an attack of Tory fever with more unani pills And a little Naure Dose He will. –30 June

The Hindustan Times, Friday, May 26, 1946

SAY ENCORE

That the Cabinet Mission's latest statement, clarifying certain points leaves the position where it was, is the opinion held in Congress circles in New Delhi, according to an Agency message.

Hindustan Times, May 28, 1946

HEAT WAVE AGAIN IN DELHI

The Hindustan Times, Wednesday, June 5, 1946.

ACCUSED THAT DELIVERS JUDGEMENT

Sir Edward Benthall, War Transport Member, stated at a Press conference at Calcutta that the Government of India must retain in its hand the ultimate control in connection with the Adjudicator's award and the Government was the final judge in the matter."

The Hindustan Times, Tuesday, June 11, 1946.

A LITTLE SACRIFICE, PLEASE!

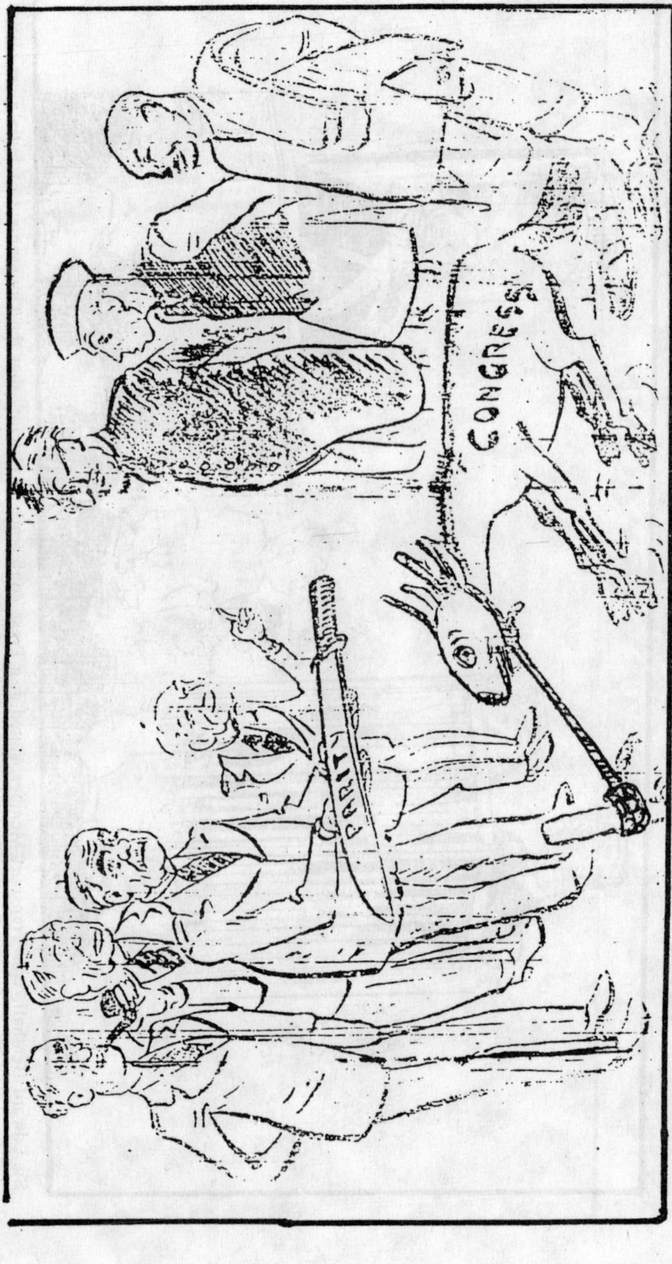

The Hindustan Times, Friday, June 14, 1946.

TRY, TRY, TRY AGAIN

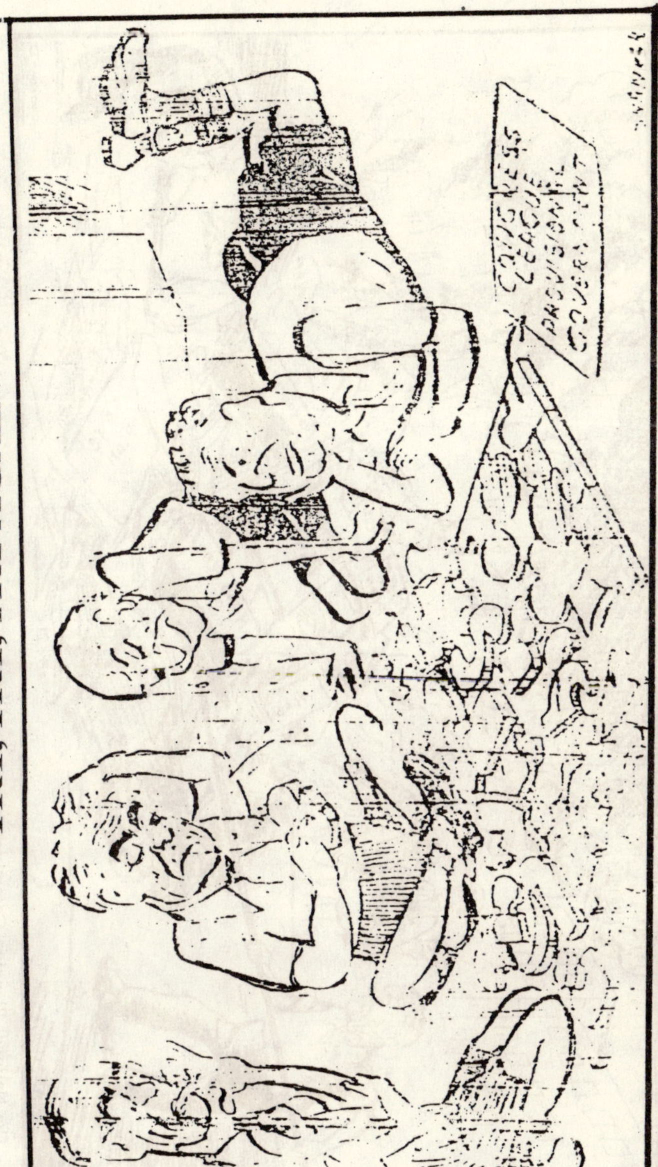

Congress League Provisional Government
The Hindustan Times, Friday, June 15, 1946.

SCORCHED EARTH PLAN

The National Planning Committee has condemned the Government's action in abolishing the Planning Department.

The Hindustan Times, Thursday, July 11, 1946.

The Hindustan Times, Thursday, July 21, 1946.

DIRECT ACTION BEGINS!

Mr. Churchill, Leader of the Opposition in the House of Commons, is reported to be taking steps to oppose the Labour Government's India policy.

Hindustan Times, August 4, 1946

DARKNESS ALL ROUND

"I am afraid the siutation remains as it was and we are where we were." – Jinnah

The Hindustan Times, Wednesday, August 14, 1946.

HELP, HELP ! THEY'RE PLANNING TO SINK US

"It is quite clear that the intervention of the Viceroy is being sought to over throw the League Ministry by alienating the sympathy of its supporters." — Hidayatullah

The Hindustan Times, Tuesday, September 10, 1946.

COLD WEATHER PESTS-I

The Hindustan Times, Tuesday, November 26, 1946.

IMAGINARY STUMBLING-BLOCK

As the talks appeared to be nearing their end, Mr. Attlee succeeded in bringing the Indian leaders together with Britain's representatives at a round table conference.

The Hindustan Times, December 08, 1946.

GOING MY WAY?

"I visualize a time when no Muslim will be in the Congress at no distant future and when that time comes we shall have to acknowledge our debt to Sardar Patel. The plight of Nationalist Muslims is rapidly becoming intolerable." - *Raja Ghazanfar Ali*

The Hindustan Times, Thursday, December 12, 1946.

NON-STOP TO INDEPENDENCE

The Hindustan Times, Wednesday, December 18, 1946.

FIRST AID — LAST AID?

Latest Resolution, Leagues resolution to boycott Constituent Assembly, Direct Action

The Hindustan Times, Tuesday, February 4, 1947.

RENDERED INNOCUOUS

The Hindustan Times, Thursday, March 27, 1947.

The Hindustan Times, June 8, 1947.

TREE PLANTING

Delhi's Tree Planting Week commences today with a demonstration of Tree-Planting organized by the Deputy Commissioner, in the grounds of Purana Qila.

The Hindustan Times, Friday, June 20, 1947.

The Hindustan Times, June 29, 1947.

THE SUN, THE MOON AND THE FLYING SAUCERS

"We do not propose to recognize the States as separate international entities on August 15." – Sir Hartley Shawcross
The Hindustan Times, Thursday, July 17, 1947.

PUNCH-AND-JUDY SHOW

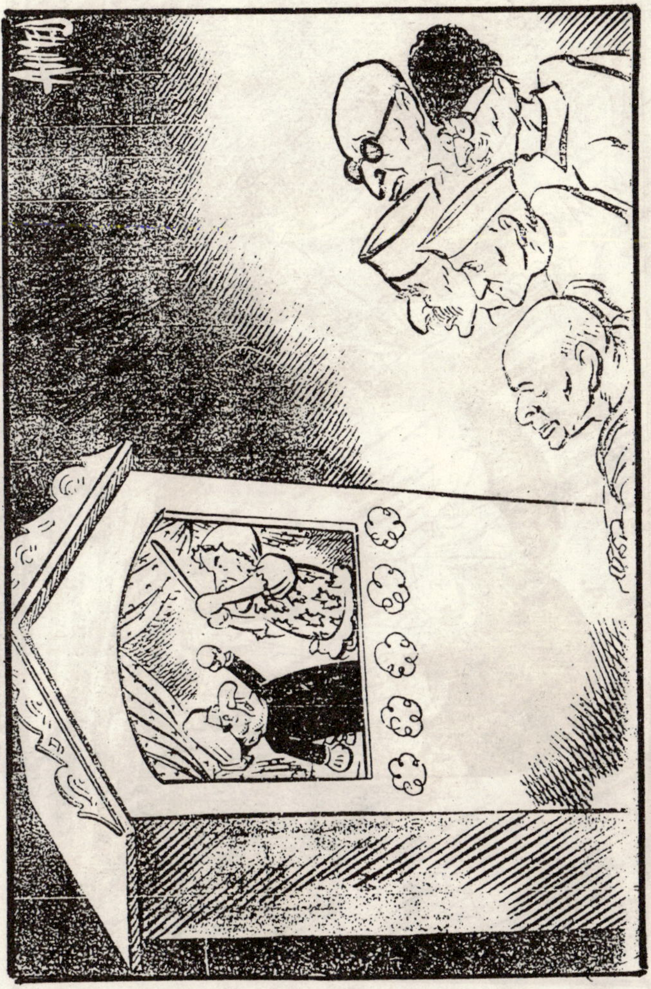

Sir C. P. Ramaswamy Iyer again met Lord Mountbatten on Tuesday
The Hindustan Times, Thursday, July 24, 1947.

"MAY WE COME IN NOW?"

Travancore has decided to accede to the Indian Dominion

The Hindustan Times, Thursday, July 31, 1947.

TO THOSE WHO SERVE

Congress leaders will be blessed by Delhi ladies prior to their departure for the Constituent Assembly on the night of August 14, by marking "mangal tilak" on their foreheads.

The Hindustan Times, Thursday, August 14, 1947.

OUT OF THE WILDERNESS

The Hindustan Times, August 15, 1947.

THOSE WHO HAVE LED THE NATION

The Hindustan Times, Independence Number, August 15, 1947.

The Hindustan Times, Indepence Number, August 15, 1947.

The Hindustan Times, August 17, 1947.

"WITH THESE RINGS . . . !"

The Committee on minorities report was debated in the Constituent Assembly and the motion for joint electorates was passed unanimously.

The Hindustan Times, Friday, August 29, 1947.

The Hindustan Times, August 31, 1947.

THE LEOPARD CHANGES ITS SPOTS

A change in the attitude of the Hyderabad Delegation is believed to have given a hopeful turn to the negotiations now proceeding.

The Hindustan Times, Tuesday, October 14, 1947.

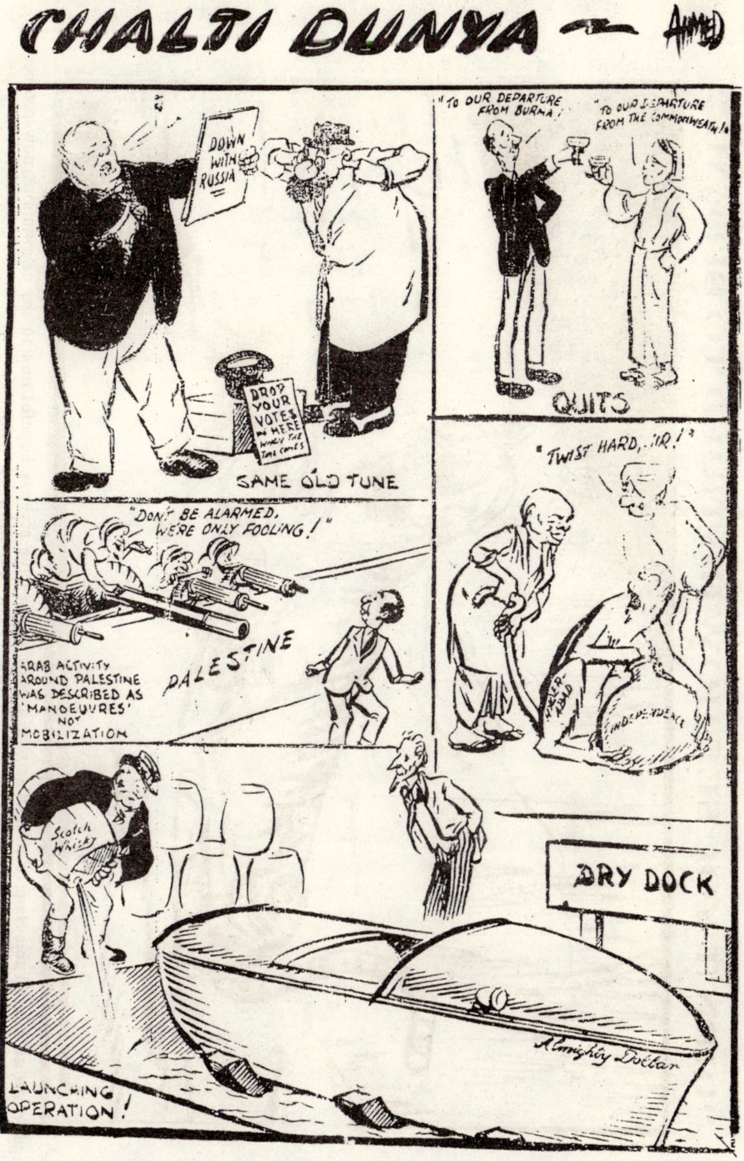

The Hindustan Times, Tuesday, October 19, 1947.

"DIDN'T YOU SEE HOW HE TRIED TO BITE ME?

Mr. Jinnah's latest telegram to the Ruler of Kashmir accuses the state authorities of opening fire on Pakistan troops

The Hindustan Times, October 28, 1947.

The Hindustan Times, November 2, 1947.

WAITER!

"If he still wants it he can come and get it himself." (On Nizam Hyderabad)

The Hindustan Times, Wednesday, June 30, 1948.

The Hindustan Times, Wednesday, July 21, 1948.

A SORE ON THE ELEPHANT'S BACK

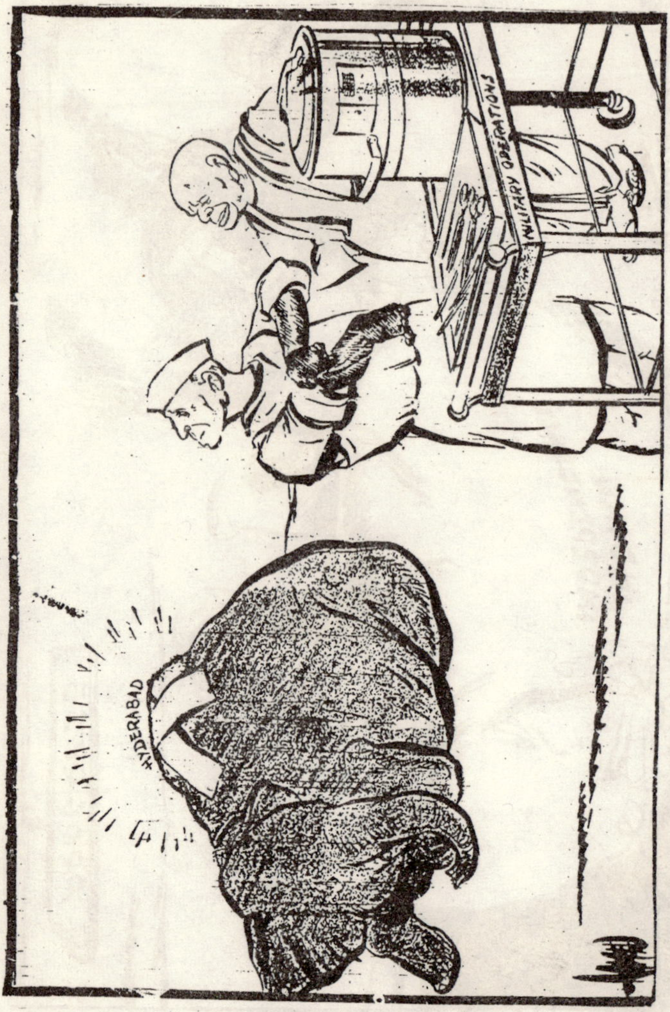

The Hindustan Times, Saturday, August 7, 1948.

The Hindustan Times, October 31, 1947.

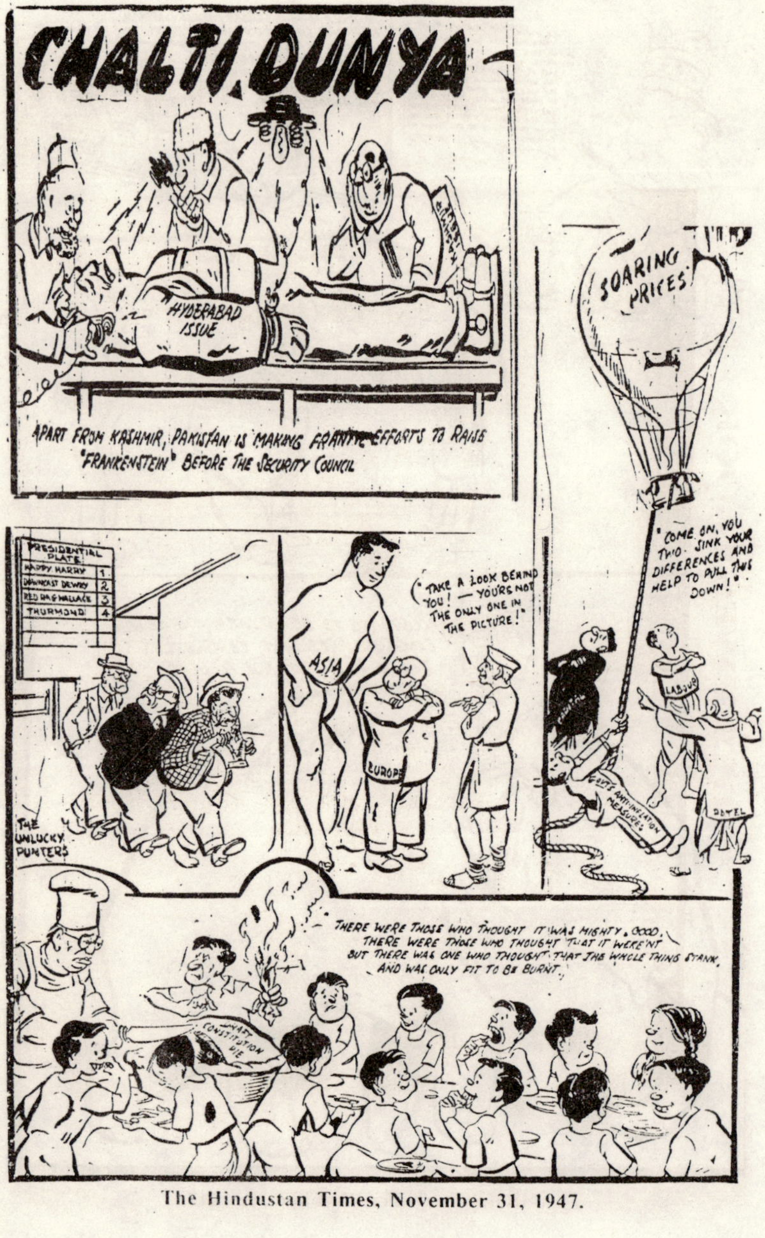

The Hindustan Times, November 31, 1947.

THE NEWEST LOOK

The Soviet Government newspaper claims that the Presidium of the National Congress has taken secret decision on dual citizenship for Indians, both Indian and British.

The Hindustan Times, Tuesday, November 23, 1948.

"India has managed to cling to unique traditions of dress, etc."

The Hindustan Times, Tuesday, November 30, 1948.

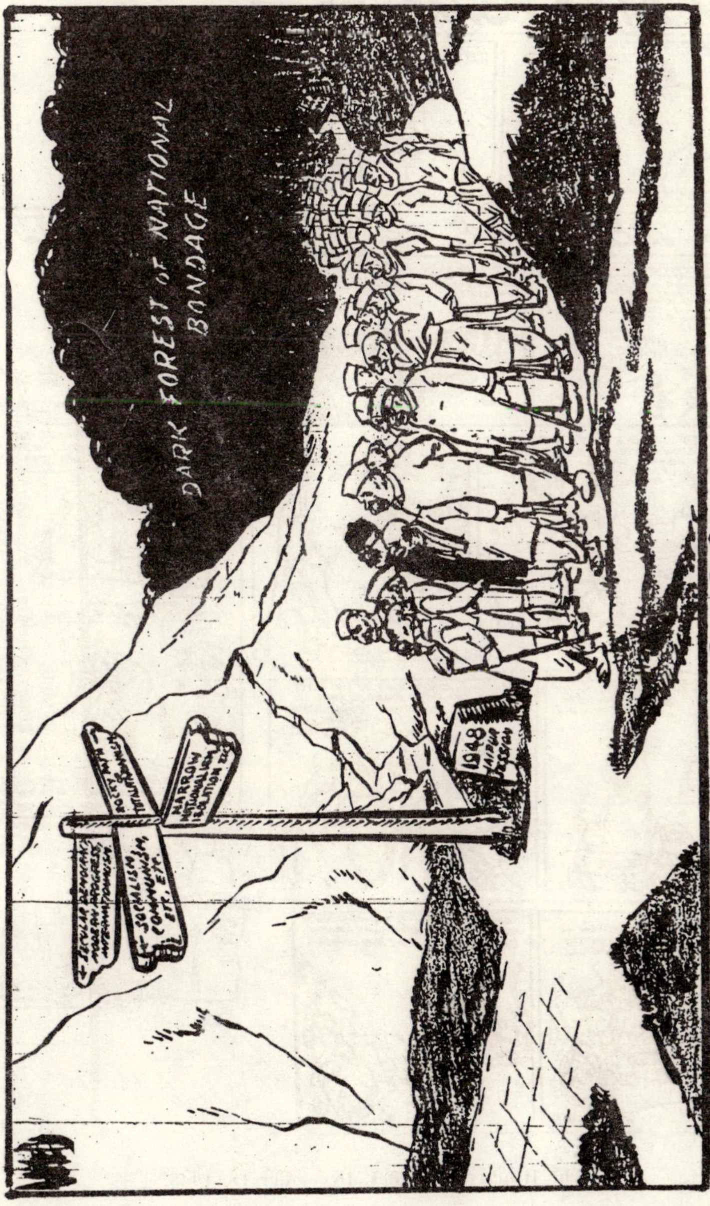

WHITHER ?

The Hindustan Times, Tuesday, December 18, 1948.

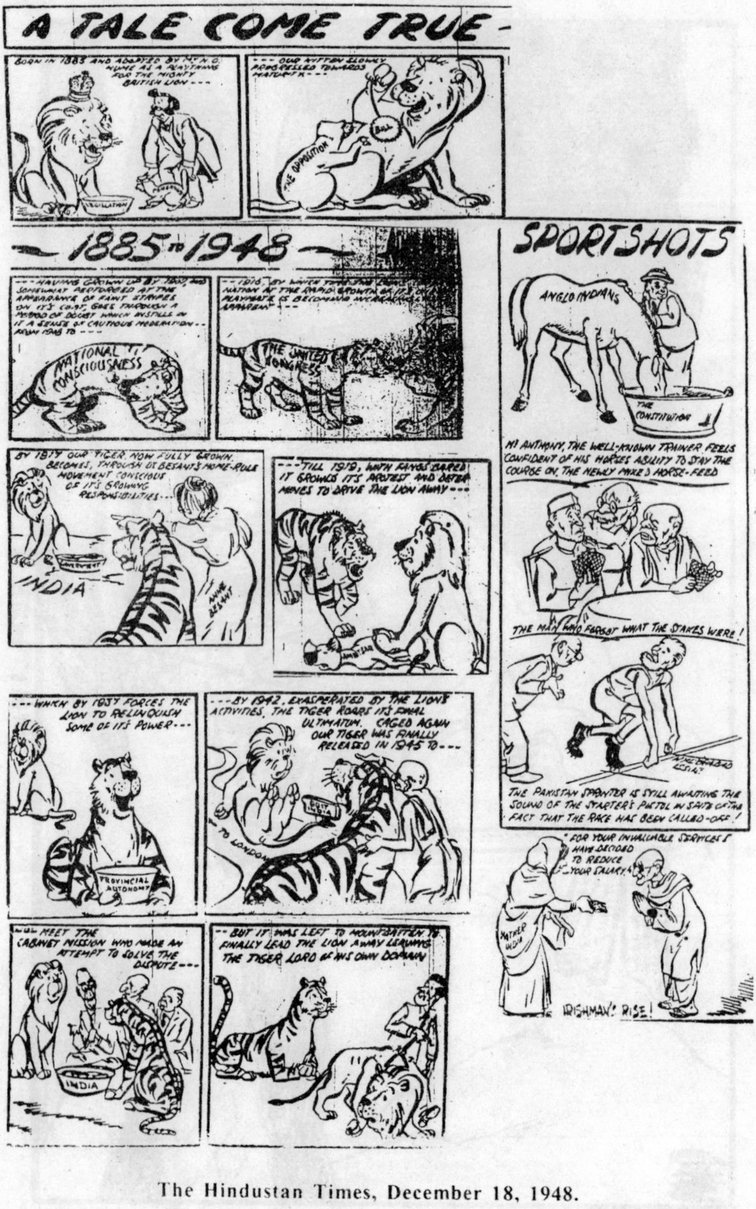

The Hindustan Times, December 18, 1948.

The Hindustan Times, December 19, 1948.

The Hindustan Times, January 30, 1949.

The Hindustan Times, February 13, 1949.

"GOOD BOYS! MOVE UP TO THE TOP OF THE CLASS!"

The Hindustan Times, February 24, 1949.

CHALTI DUNYA
"THE POOR FELLOW'S BOAT IS SINKING! YOU CANT VERY WELL EXPECT ME TO TAKE HIM TO TASK FOR THROWING OUT THE INDIAN!"
M.L.A

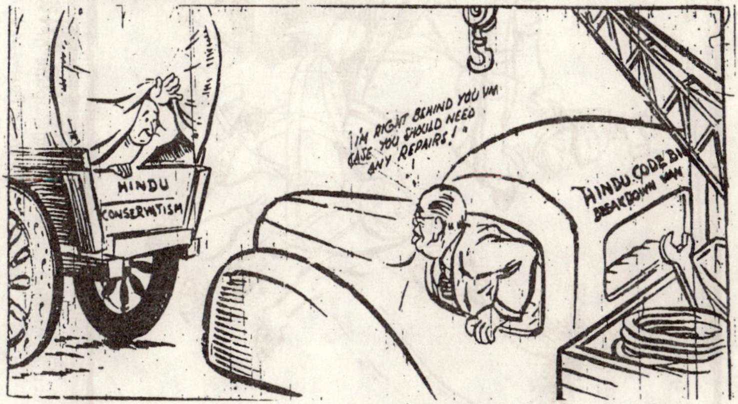
"I'M RIGHT BEHIND YOU IN CASE YOU SHOULD NEED ANY REPAIRS!"
HINDU CONSERVATISM
HINDU CODE BI
BREAKDOWN VAN

SPORTSHOTS
SARDAR PATEL HAS JUST RETURNED FROM A GAME OF CHESS IN HYDERABAD. IT IS REPORTED THAT THE GAME WAS NOT FOR HIGH STAKES!

NO HORSE-SENSE

Sardar Patel addressing Congressmen at Ambala deprecated indiscipline in Congress ranks with particular reference to decisions amongst Congress Party M.L.A.s.

The Hindustan Times, Tuesday, March 8, 1949.

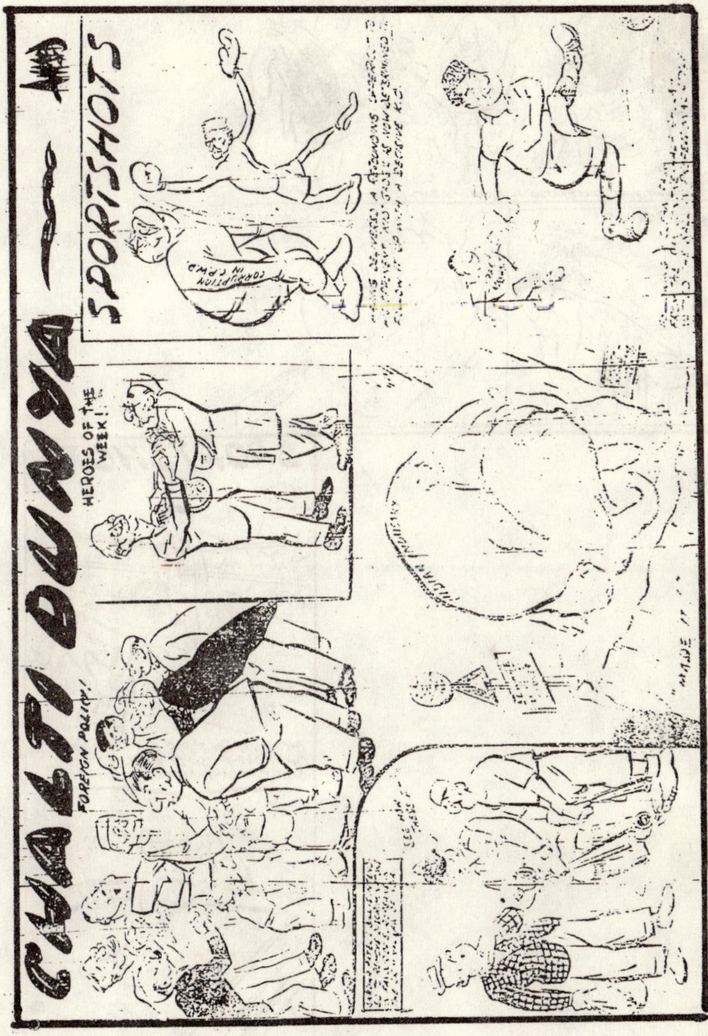

The Hindustan Times, March 13, 1949.

The Hindustan Times, March 20, 1949.

The Hindustan Times, April 10, 1949.

ONWARD, COMMONWEALTH SOLDIERS!

"It should not be difficult to fit a Republic into the framework of the Commonwealth", Pandit Nehru told a "Daily Mail" correspondent. On the question of Commonwealth defence he said : "It would not be in the interests of India to engage herself in any pact that would automatically involve her in war."

The Hindustan Times, Wednesday, April 13, 1949.

ACHIEVEMENT

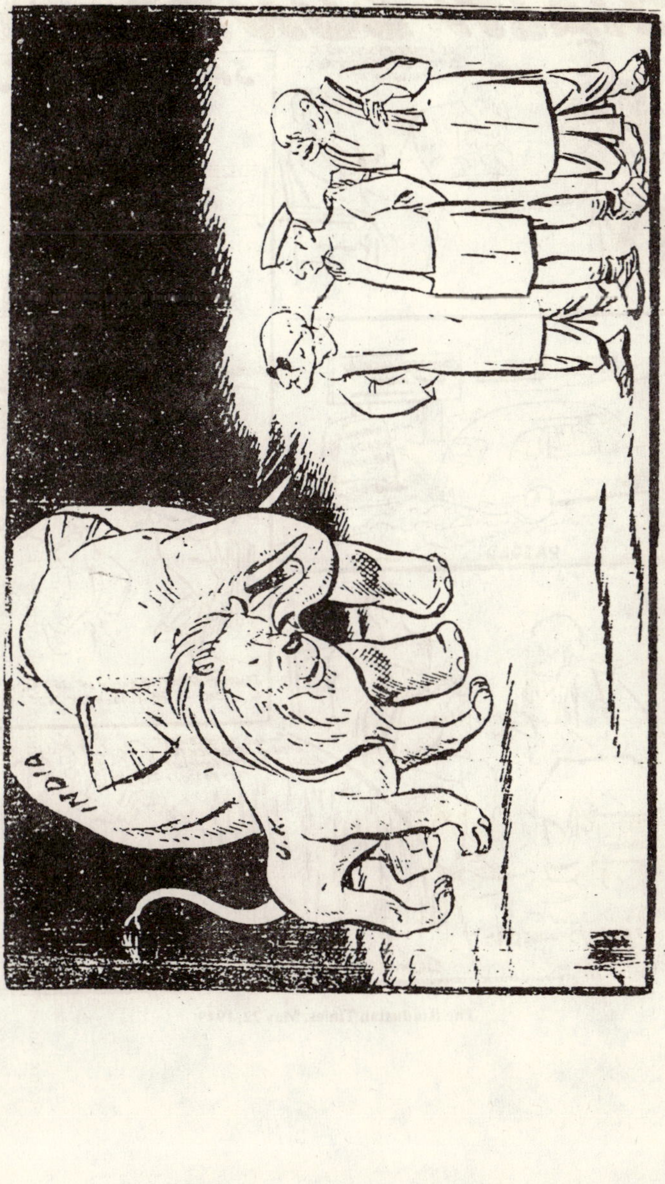

The Hindustan Times, Saturday, May 7, 1949.

The Hindustan Times, May 22, 1949

The Hindustan Times, June 12, 1949

The Hindustan Times, June 12, 1949

LEST WE FORGET

August 15, 1948 to Aug 1949 (A Year of Achievement)
The Hindustan Times

ATTENTION, BOYS!

" If we reflect ----- Sardar Patel in his Independence Day's Message to the Nation.

The Himestan Times, August 17, 1949

RIDING INSTRUCTORS ?

The Hindustanl Times, October 12, 1949

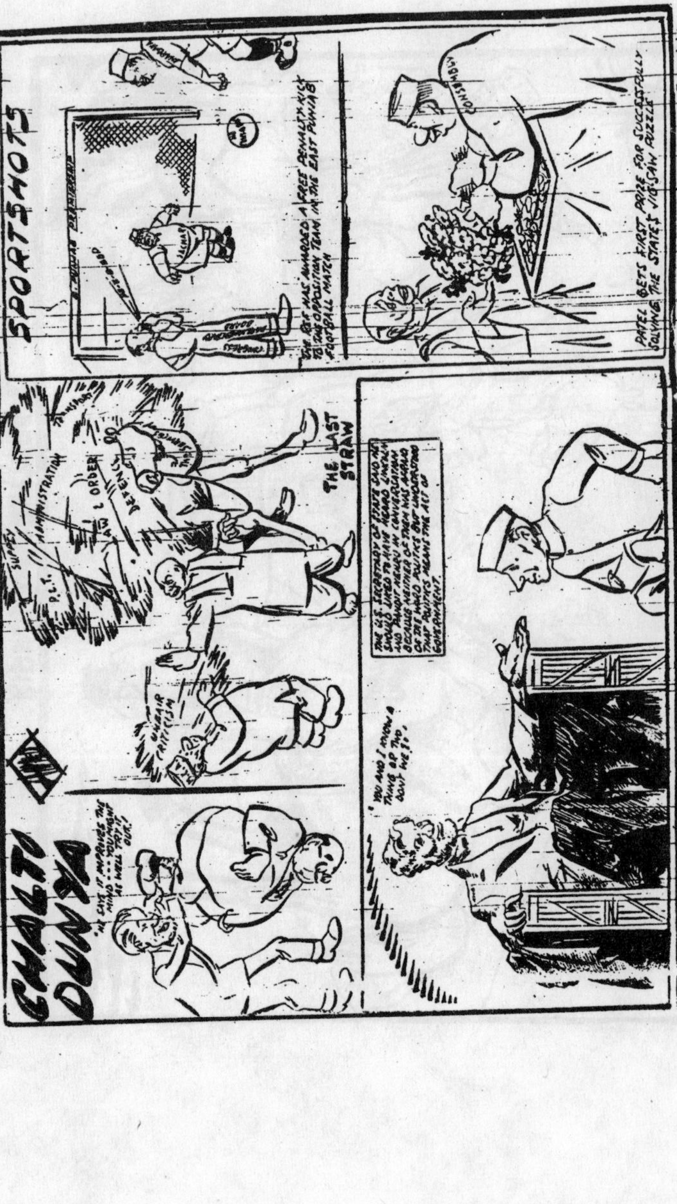

The Hindustan Times, October 16, 1949

GULLIVER GETS A BREAK

The Hindustan Times, Wednesday, November 16, 1949.

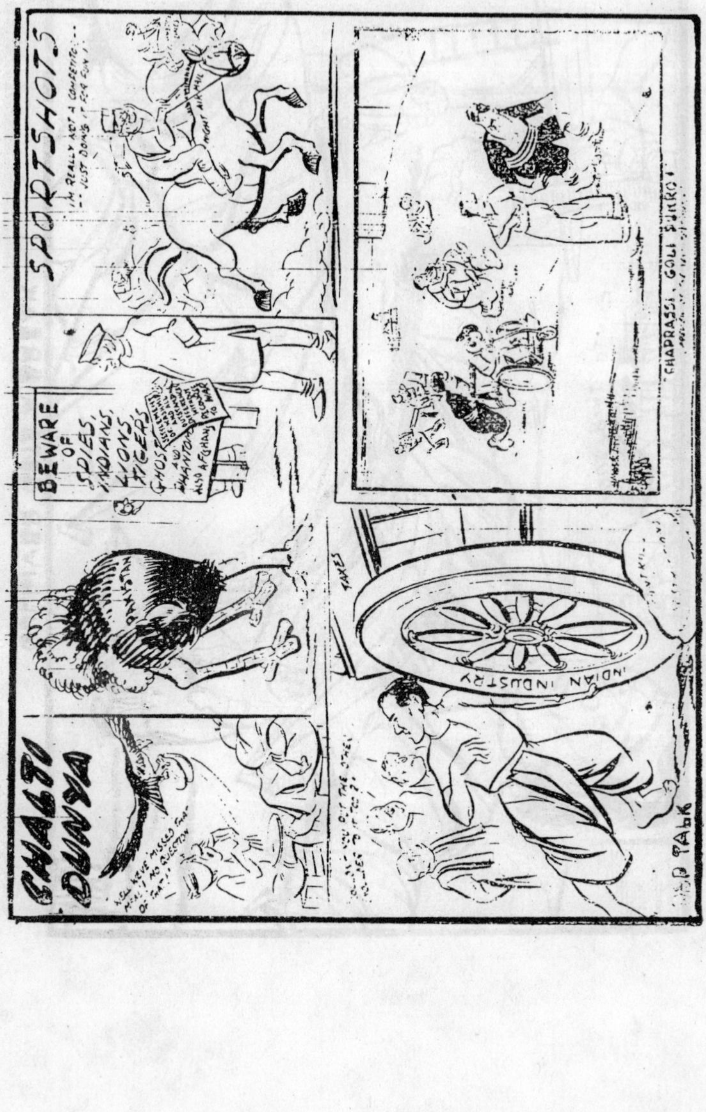

The Hindustan Times, November 20, 1949.

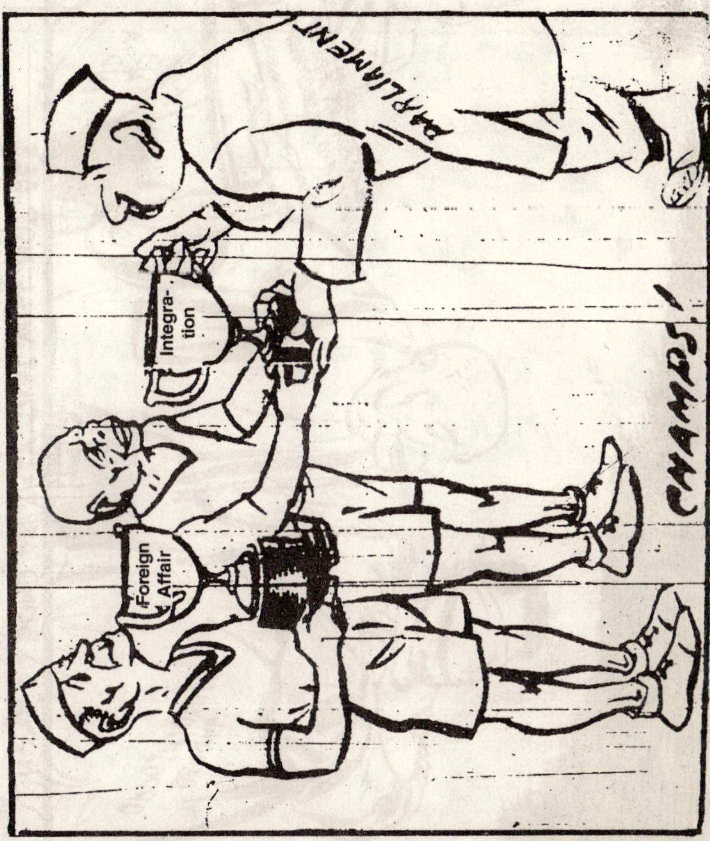

The Hindustan Times, Sunday, February 5, 1950.

NONE SO BLIND AS THEY THAT WILL NOT SEE

The Hindustan Times, Tuesday, April 18, 1950.

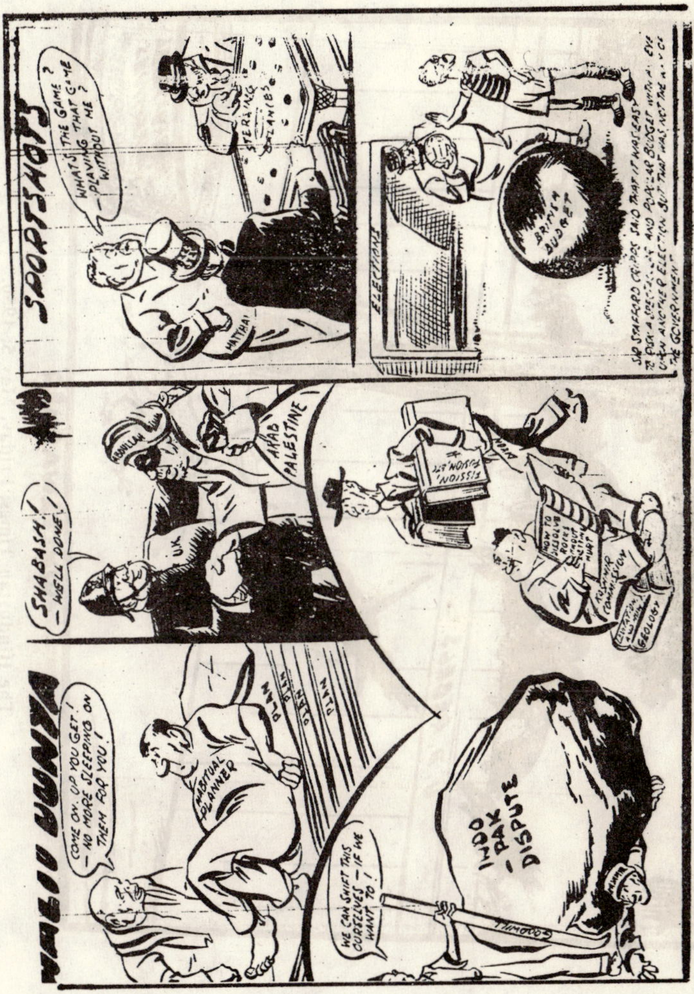

The Hindustan Times, Tuesday, April 30, 1950.

WHITEWASHED

The Hindustan Times, Friday, May 5, 1950.

15th AUGUST

THREE-YEAR-OLD SAPLING

The Hindustan Times, August 15, 1950.

The Hindustan Times, August 20, 1950.

"STEEL FRAME" LIQUIDATION AND AFTER

The Bombay Chronicle, Vol. XXXV, No. 13, January 16, 1947.

TUG OF (COLD) WAR

The Bombay Cronicle, Vol. XXXVI, No. 146, June 23, 1948.

THE LUNATIC AT LARGE

"NOTHING BUT CRIMINAL LUNACY IN BRITAIN COULD POSSIBLY DESTROY INDIA'S GOODWILL TOWARDS HER"

—MOUNTBATTEN

The Bombay Cronicle, Vol. XXXVI, No. 154, July 2, 1948.

PEACE SEEKER

The Nizam, according to the latest reports, is seeking to have the June 17 offer reopened.
The Bombay Chronicle, Vol. XXXVI, No. 184, Friday, August 6, 1948.

GULLIVER AWAKES

In the age of aeroplane when feudalism and sovereignties are anachronisms, the Government of India, as the dominant Power in India responsible for the defence and general security of the country, cannot be expected to admit the Nizam's claim to independence; more so when it has no sanction of the will of the people behind it and comes only from the Nizam — whose attitude, to quote from the British resident at Hyderabad in 1926, 'leaves but a faint hope that he would, if he realises his dreams of unchecked absolutism, consider the welfare of his people in the least degree — and the handful at the peak of his feudal pyramid". Hyderabad White Paper.

The Bombay Chronicle, Vol. XXXVI, No. 188, August 11, 1948.

APPEARANCE AND REALITY

The Bombay Chronicle, Vol XXXVII No46 Feb 24, 1949

'People say I have removed the Crown from the Maharajas. It is wrong. I have only removed the dirt from their crowns'—Sardar Patel at Madras.

The Bombay Chronicle, Vol. XXXVII, No. 046, February 24, 1949.

The Bombay Chronicle, Vol. XXXXVII, No. 085, April 11, 1949.

THE HALL OF FAME

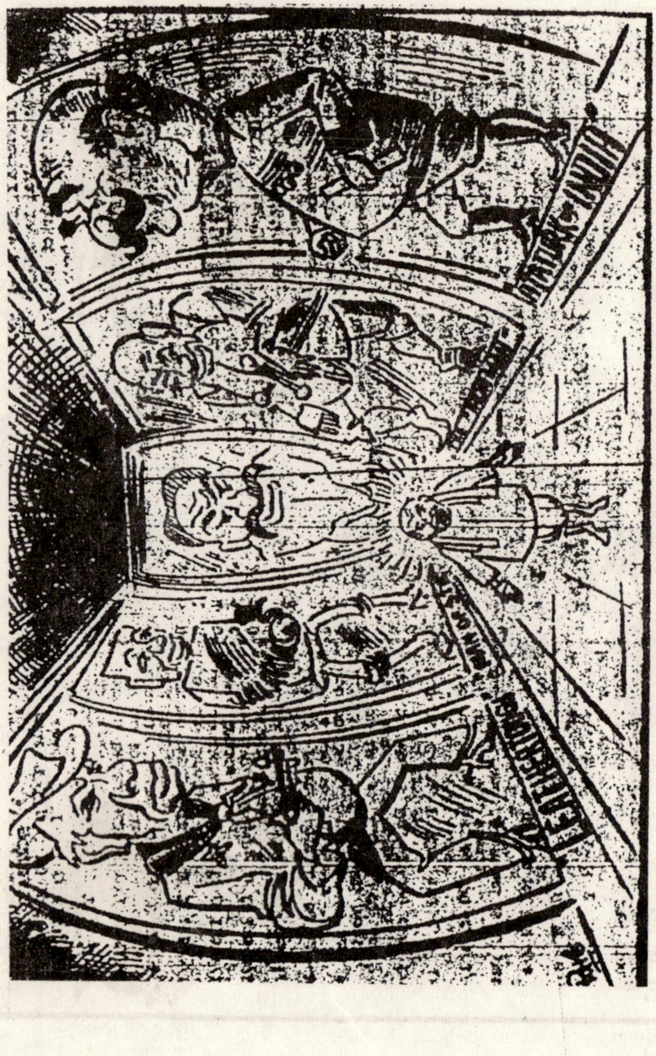

The Bombay Chronicle, May 9, 1949.

From L to R. Leather Tough; Man of Steel; The Iron Team; Atantuk of India

HATS OFF TO NEW ORDER

No more seats will "reserved", according to a motlon adopted by the Constituent Assembly.

The Bombay Chronicle Vol. XXXVII, No. 127, Monday, May 30, 1949.

BIOGRAPHY

AUTHOR	TITLE	PRICE
Athavale, P	My Story An Autobiography of Hindu Widow	175/-
Bakshi, S.R.	Gandhi & Ideology of Swadeshi	150/-
Chattopadhyay, Anjana	Encyclopaedia of Indian Scientists (From Ancient to Contemporary)	395/-
Chopra, P.N.	Maulana Azad: Selected Speeches & Statements 1940-1947.	200/-
Chopra, P.N.	The Receding Horizons- A Historian's Reminiscences	225/-
Chopra, P.N., Chopra Prabha	Sardar Patel In Cartoons	
Erickson, Paul. A.	Anthropological Lives - Biographies of Eminent Anthropologists.	175/-
Homchaudhuri. S,	Keats- A Reading Of His Major Poems	150/-
Jaspal, Brig Pratap Singh	Samast Ilahi Jot -Baba Nand Singhji Maharaj Punjabi Part -1	75/-
Jaspal, Brig Pratap Singh	Samast Illahi Jot- Baba Nand Singhji Maharaj Punjabi Part-II	75/-
Jaspal, Brig Pratap Singh	Samast Illahi Jot- Baba Nand Singhji Maharaj Punjabi Part-III	75/-
Jaspal, Brig Pratap Singh	Sada Jagrit Jyoti Prakash Hi Prakash Baba Nand Singhji Maharaj (Kaleran Wale) Part -1	75/-
Jaspal, Brig Pratap Singh	Shahidan De Sartaj Guru Arjan Partak Har	20/-
	Gobind Prem - Guru Gobind Singhji And The Khalsa (Punjabi)	20/-
Jaspal, Brig Pratap Singh	Eternal Glory of Guru Amar Dasji	35/-
Jaspal, Brig Pratap Singh	Eternal Glory of Guru Gobind Singhji And The Khalsa	125/-
Jaspal, Brig Pratap Singh	Eternal Glory of Baba Nand Singhji Maharaj	75/--
Kohli, A.B.	Councils of Ministers In India	295/-
Kohli, A.B.	Directory of Union Ministers 1947 - 1987	125/-
Kohli, A.B.	Encyclopedia of Central Ministers in India	295/-

Kohli, A.B.	Govt. of India - Nehru to Narasimha Rao	250/-
Kohli, A.B	Presidents of India (2nd Edition)	225/-
Kohli, A.B.	Titans of Indian Politics	295/-
Kohli, Anil	Shekhar: Statements, Policies & Opinions	350/-
Kunju, N	Unknown Soldier and Other Poems	85/-
Lajpat Rai	Swamy Dayanand Saraswati	125/-
Maprayil, Cyriac	Bangabandhu-Sheikh Mujibur Rahman	135/-
Mukherjee, A.G.	Jawaharlal Nehru :	400/-
& Tagra, Vinod	Architect of Modern India	
Murthi, R.K.	Jawaharlal Nehru: Glimpses of Greatness	200/-
& Parashar, Rajan		
Padmanabhan, Neela	Poems By Neelapadmanabhan	125/-
Palit, D.K. Maj. Gen Vr. C.	Major General AA Rudra	350/-
Rai, Lt Gen H.C.	Memories Still Linger	325/-
Rama Rao, V.V.B.	Graham Green's Comic Vision	175/-
Sharma, Gautam Lt. Col.	Soldier's Memoirs (Army Narratives)	195/-
Sharma S. & Sharma Indra	Encylopedia of Women in Sports	395/-
Sharma S. & Sharma Indra	Directory of Chief Ministers of India	250/-
Sharma S & Sharma Indra	Directory of Governors Of India	
Sinha, B.M.	Epochal Men	200/-
Tagra, Vinod	Jawaharlal Nehru And The Status of	
	Women In India-Analytical Study	
Tony Mains And Elizabeth	Rifleman To Colonel - Memoirs of Major	
Talbot Rice	Gajendra Malla 9th Gorkha Rifles	175/-
Tulsiram, Nand Lal	Imagery in Tulsidasa's Ramcharitmanas	175/-
Venkataramani, K.S.	My Pial Teacher & Other Stories From	
	South-India	175/-